Happy Hands Writing Practice
Tracing Letters & Numbers, Ages 4-6
Just like in School!

by Mary Drewry, Teacher K-6
& Patricia Azeltine

DIRECTIONS

1. Say the letter name out loud.
2. Have your child say the letter name out loud.
3. Have your child trace the three letters on the line.
4. Have your child write the letter three times on the same line.
5. Do this for capital and small case letters.
6. Tell your child what the picture is and ask what other words start with this letter.
7. Have him/her color the picture representing the letter.

Square #1 represents the letters that use the entire line from top to bottom.

Square #2 shows the letters written from the dotted line to the bottom line.

Square #3 describes the letters that start at the dotted line and go below the bottom line.

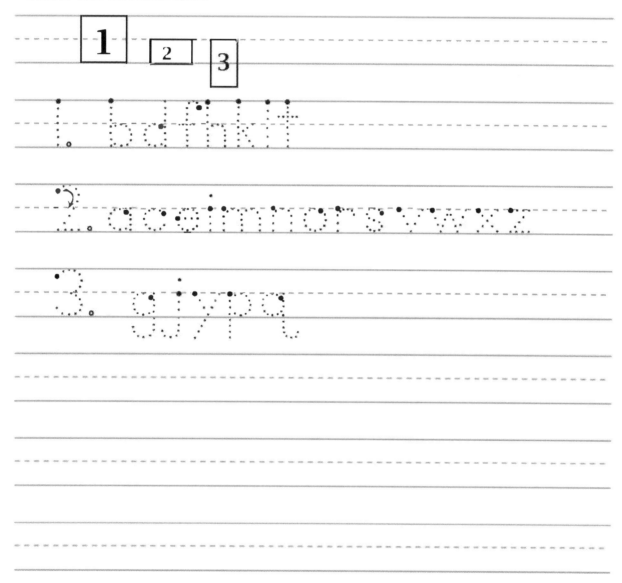

1. bdfhklt

2. aceimnors vwxz

3. gjypq

Aa

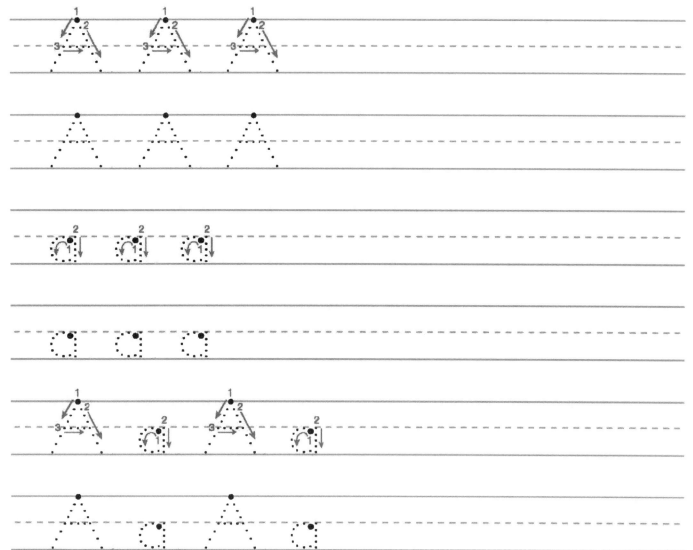

Bb

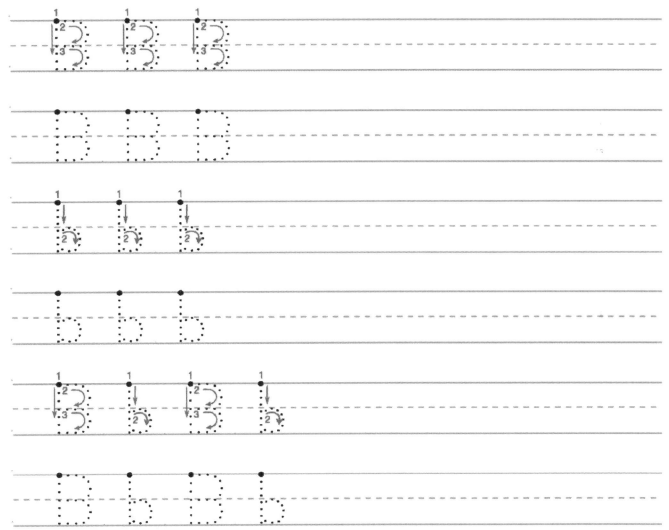

Cc

Dd

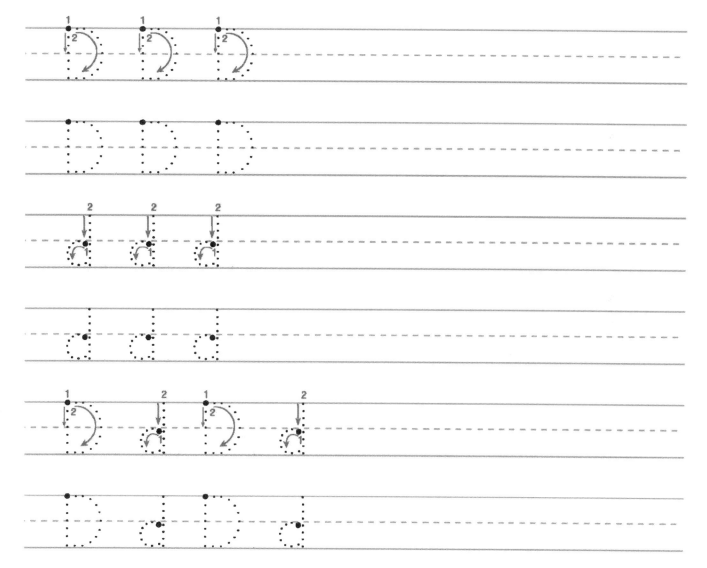

Ee

Ff

Gg

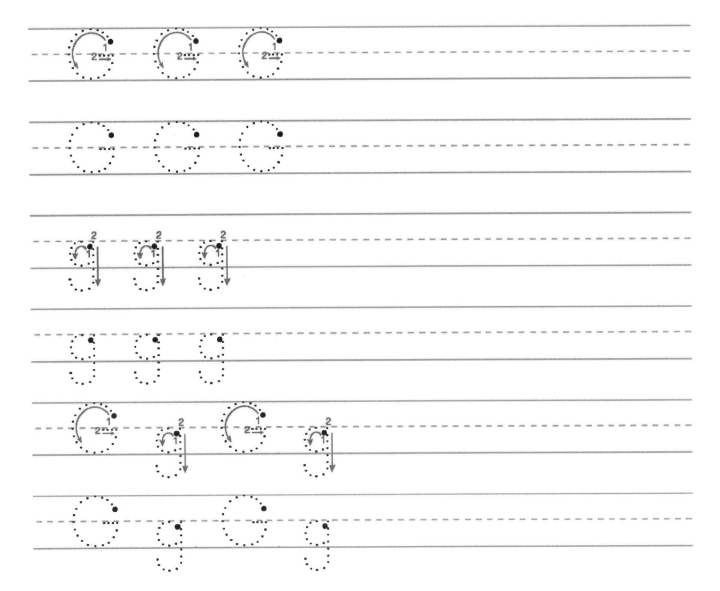

Hh

Ii

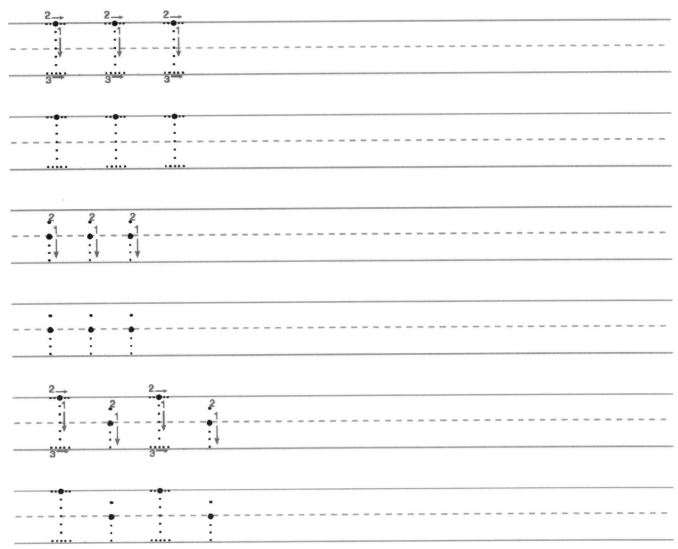

Jj

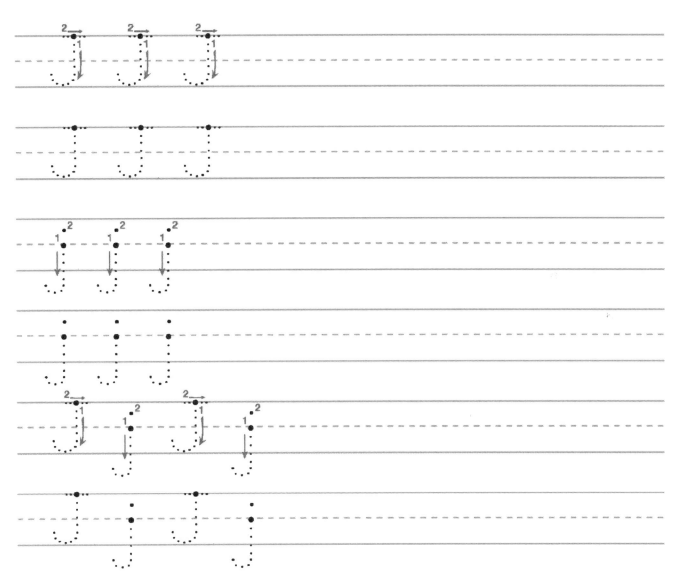

Kk

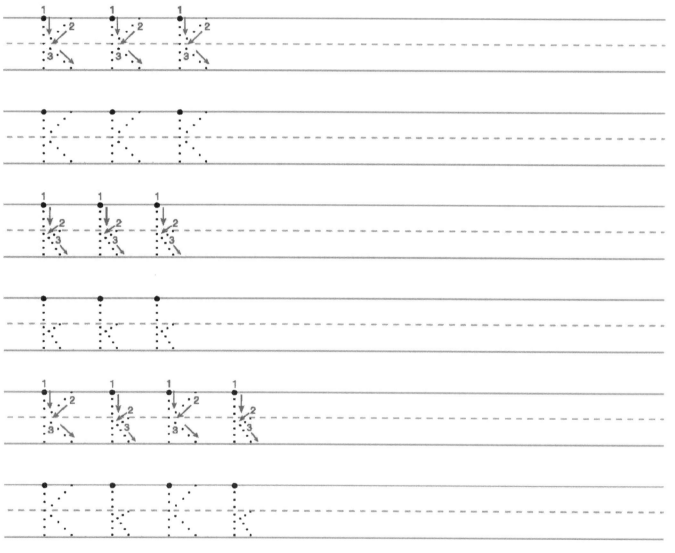

Ll

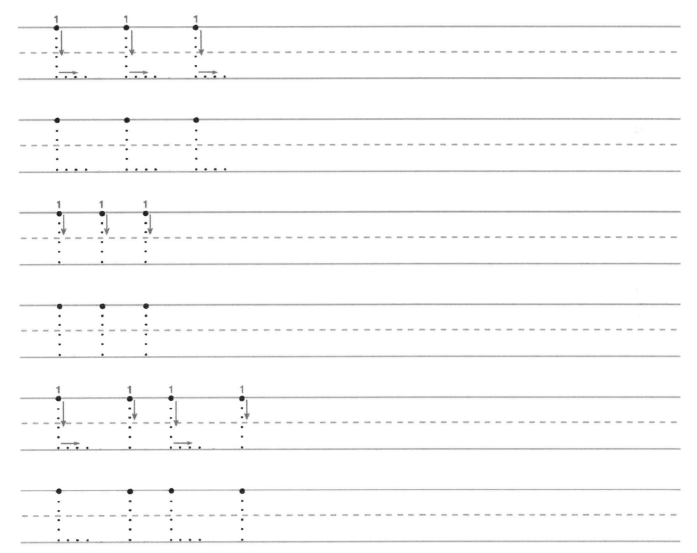

Mm

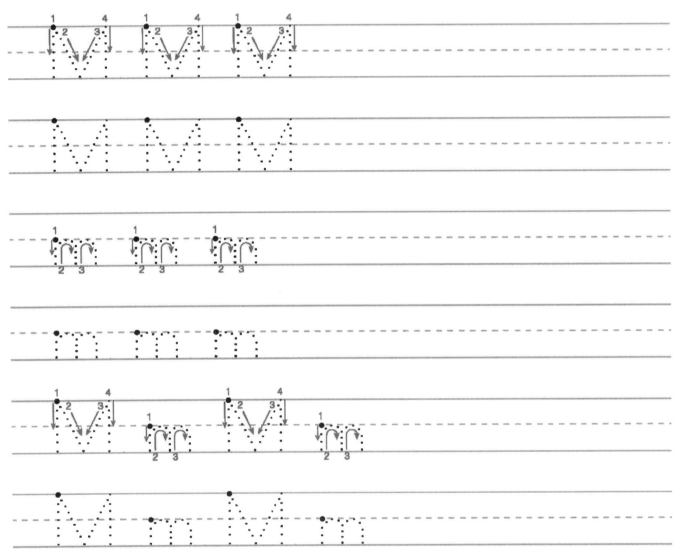

Nn

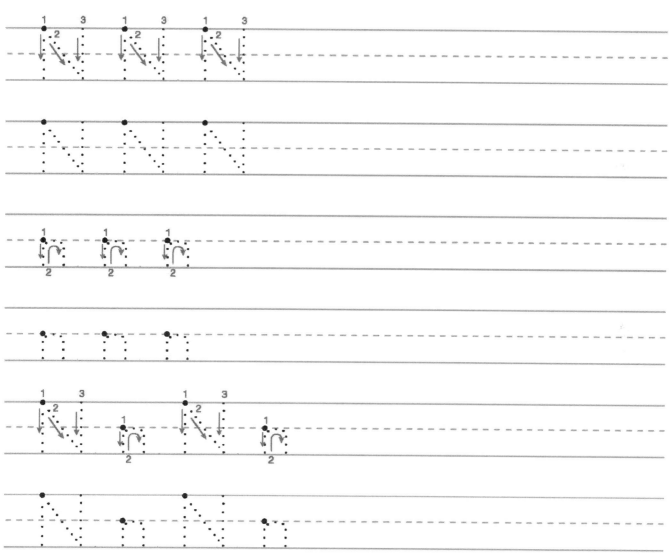

Oo

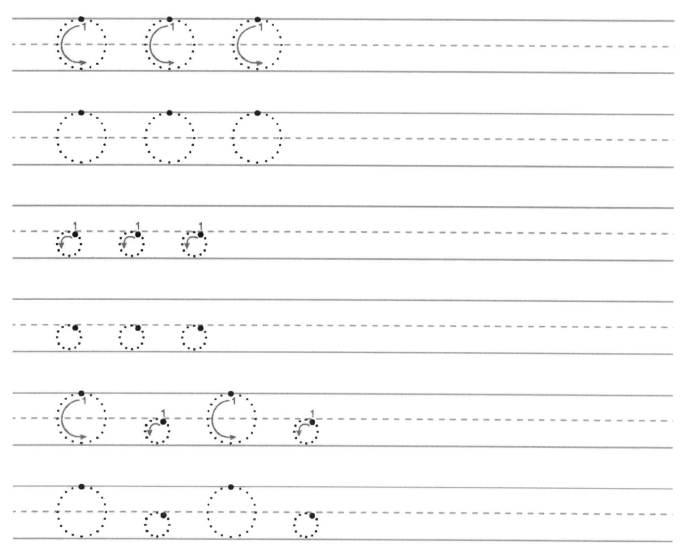

Pp

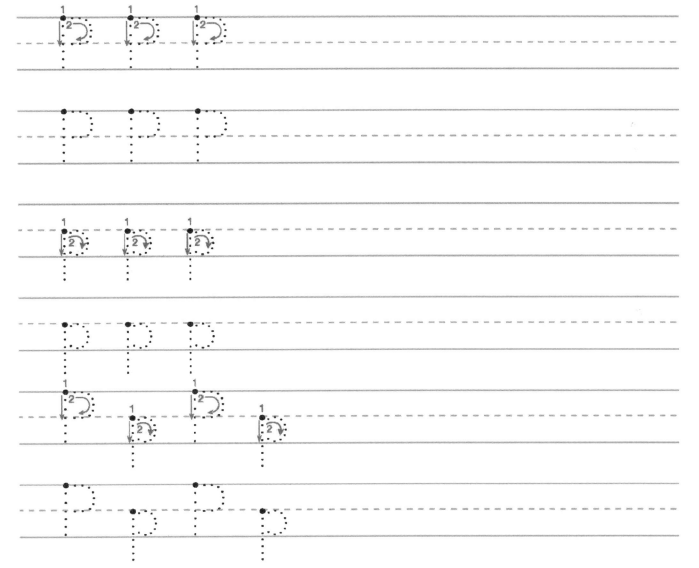

Qq

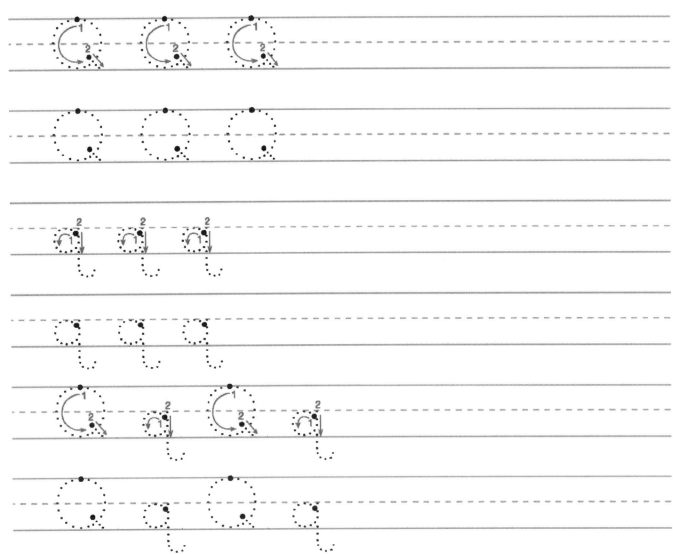

Rr

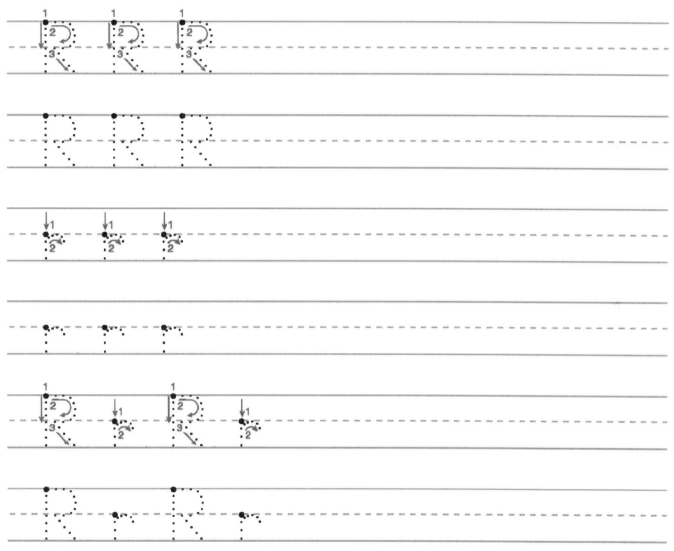

Ss

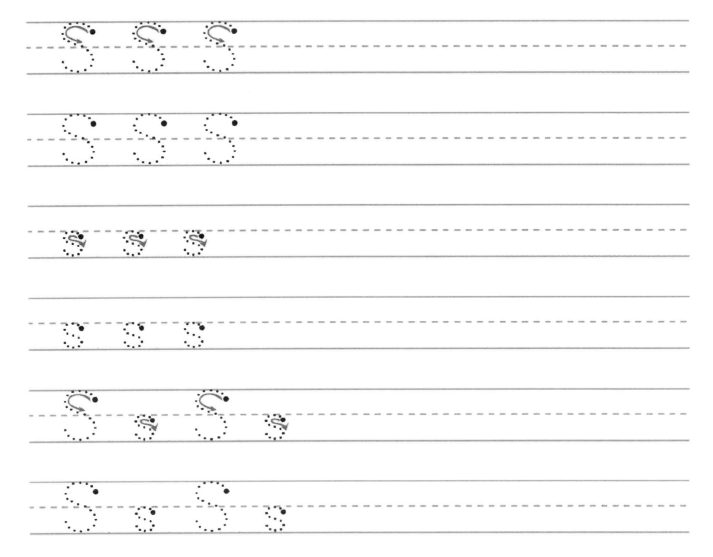

T t

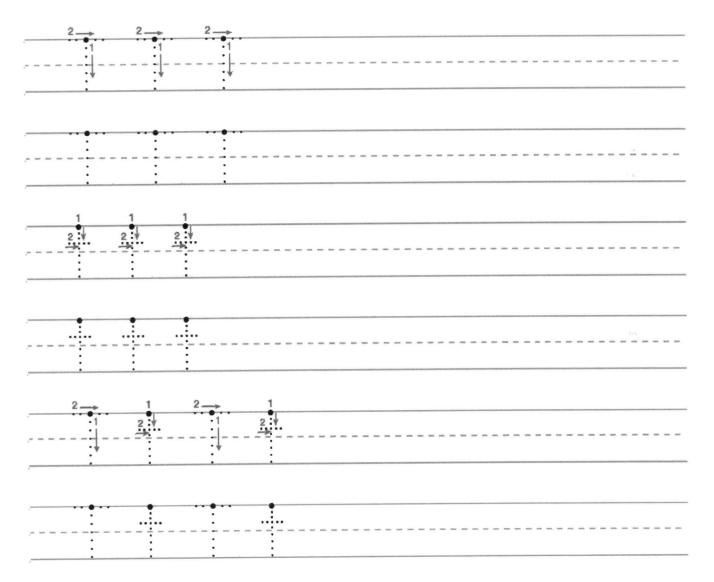

Uu

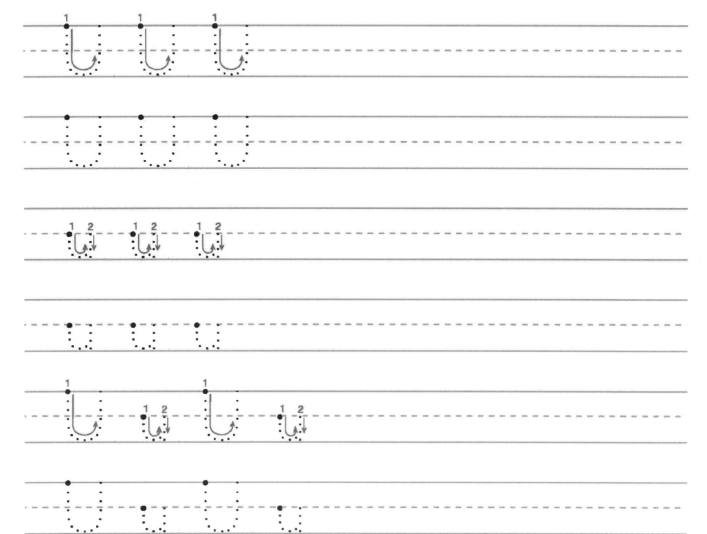

V v

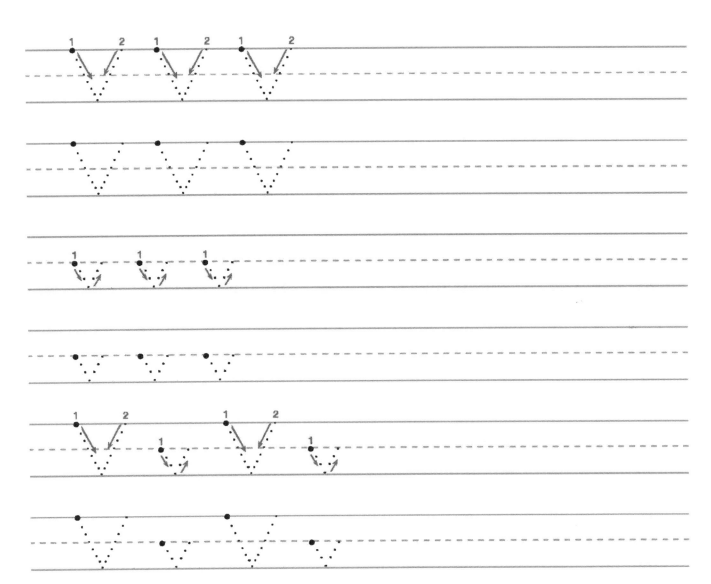

Ww

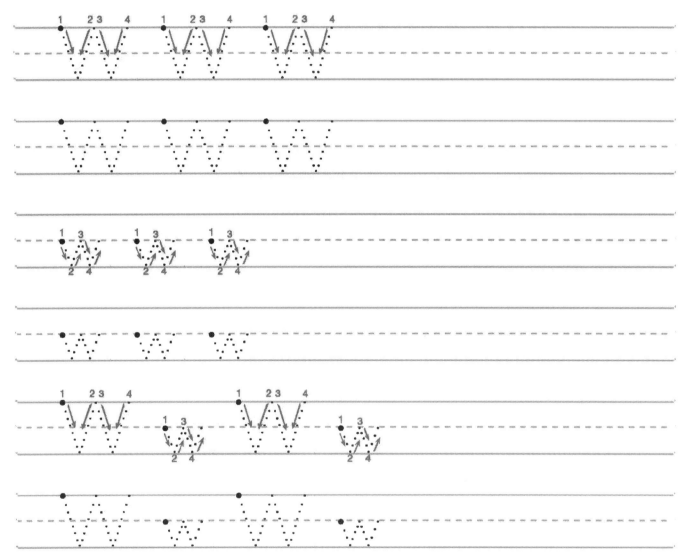

Xx

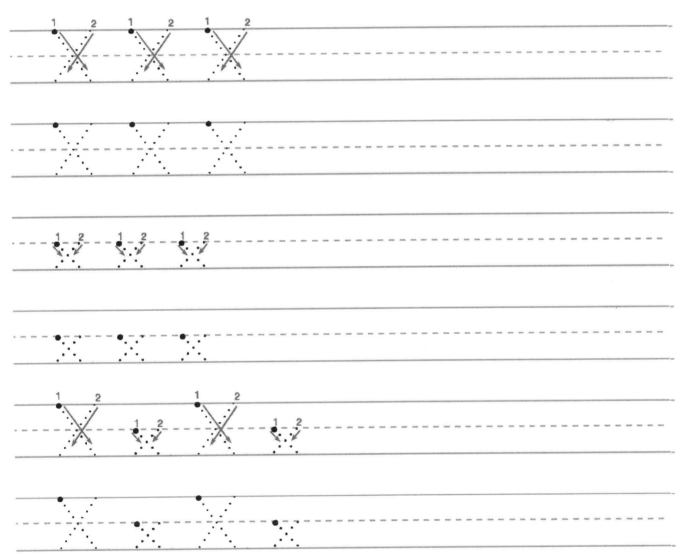

Yy

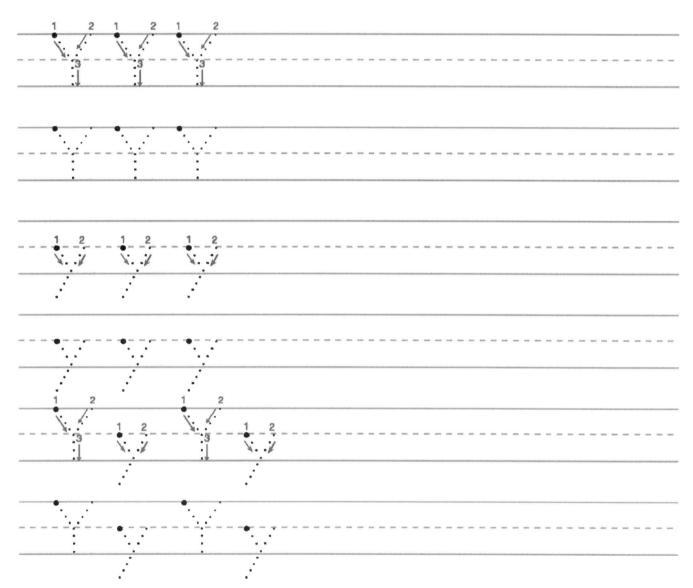

Z z

01

Trace the numbers, and draw a picture of the number in space below.

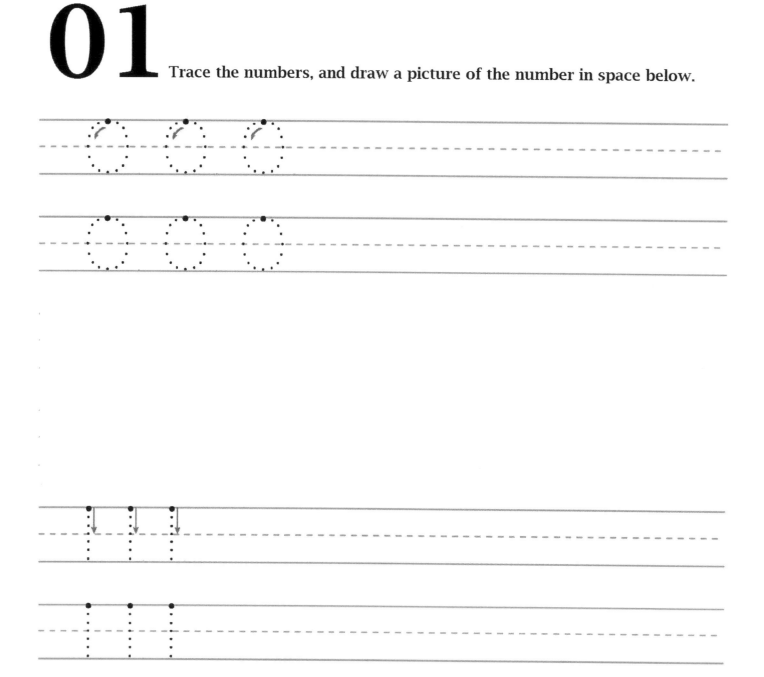

23 Trace the numbers, and draw a picture of the number in space below.

45

Trace the numbers, and draw a picture of the number in space below.

67

Trace the numbers, and draw a picture of the number in space below.

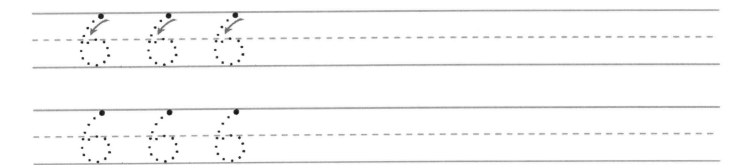

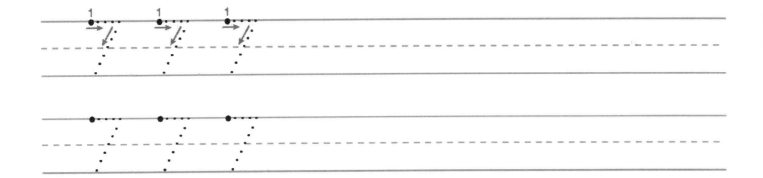

89

Trace the numbers, and draw a picture of the number in space below.

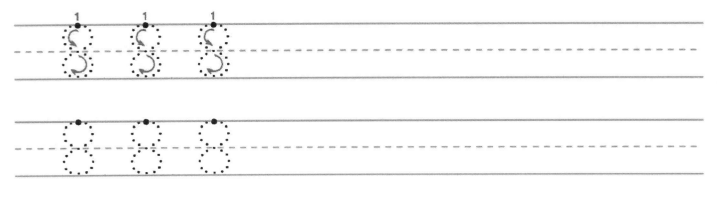

Square #1 represents the letters that use the entire line from top to bottom.

Square #2 shows the letters written from the dotted line to the bottom line.

Square #3 describes the letters that start at the dotted line and go below the bottom line.

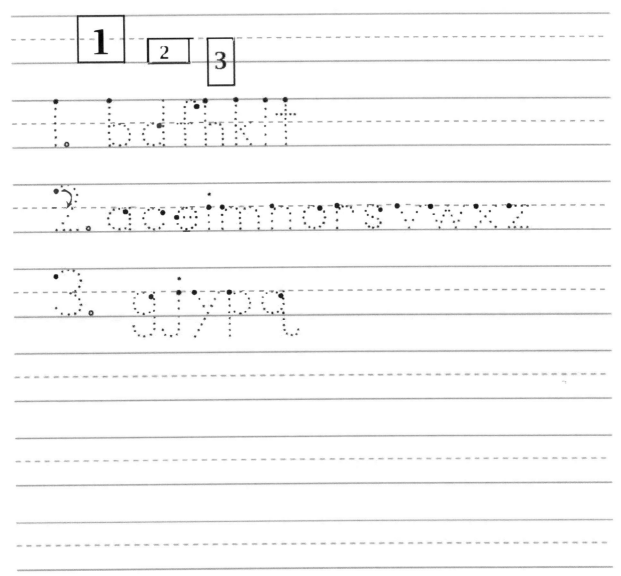

Thank you for purchasing our tracing book. If you liked this book, find more of them on Amazon or at https://www.pkburian.com/.

Proof

Made in the USA
Columbia, SC
27 May 2017